The Night I Woke Up

From Fortunate Rejections and Proud Failures to a Phenomenal Night of Reincarnation

notionpress.com

The Night I Woke Up

From Fortunate Rejections and Proud Failures to a Phenomenal Night of Reincarnation

Shweta Singh

notionpress.com

Notion Press

Old No. 38, New No. 6

McNichols Road, Chetpet

Chennai - 600 031

First Published by Notion Press 2016

ISBN 978-93-86009-53-1

This book is dedicated to the child inside you for that child has lofty dreams and everything is possible for him/her.

Contents

Preface

My love for this life cannot be expressed in words. I am grateful to this opportunity and to The Universe for having made me who I am. For being able to reach you and give you a glimpse of how beautiful your life can become, only if you allow it to.

I want you to feel the love in you and in the air you breathe.

I know this book will inspire you to live your absolute best life.

Thankyou for having the courage to pick it up.

About a year ago, I was on my way to success but filled with pain and sensing I wasn't living anything close to my authentic life and my true potential. I began a search–seeking out answers to my dreams and visions, the purpose of my existence and true & enduring happiness.

What I discovered on the way altered my life. So I decided to share everything I learned within the book you are now holding.

If I've learned a valuable lesson in life, then it's my obligation to share that with you so that you don't have to go through the same drama, struggle, or miles traveled to figure it out.

I value my life experience, my message, and my voice because I believe these things have been a gift to me. And if The Universe valued the experiences I have had in my life enough to give them to me, then I value them enough to pass them on to you.

Acknowledgements

For the creation of the book, The Night I Woke Up, I want to thank the following people for their invaluable assistance in making this book what it is:

My deepest thanks to my publishers at Notion Press.

My thanks to my wonderful parents for their unconditional love and support so that we can make a difference in the world. From the bottom of my heart, thank you mum and papa, for everything.

To my lovely sister, Upma Singh, for her spiritual light, love and encouragement, for being a phenomenal editor and for designing the superb cover page of this book.

You always have that one mentor you admire, not because you were her favorite, but because of the impact of their words leave on you. My dearest teacher Ms. Anshu Doger Gagal. I remember the day and your words to me. See, where they've landed me. Thank you.

To my dearest friends: Gursimrat Singh for he continually inspires me to greatness, for being a constant support and for his invaluable assistance, Ashish Jain who wrote the poem 'Words from a Friend' and whose faith causes me to lift myself to new levels so that I can fulfill my dreams of inspiring billions, Akanksha Gupta and Isha Dara for their never ending love and support through the good times and through the challenging times.

Wait! I forgot to introduce myself to you! What about a short journey to my journal that I kept during the time I was writing the book which actually is a series of questions I answered in response to THE MASTERY MANUAL by Robin Sharma?

I am so excited to start this journey with you!

16 November 2015

If you were asked to describe yourself in one paragraph, what would that paragraph say?

I am a soul fired by a vision to help people realize their inestimable potential. I am a limitless being born to accomplish wonders. I am here to transform all my dreams into reality.

I am a bundle of energy waving into this universe creating a revolution of transformation.

If there was one word you would want your life to stand for, what would that one word be?

Vision

What has been the value of my most painful experience and how would your life be less if you had not had the benefit of them?

The value of my most painful experience has been, it made me learn-

Be so good that people need you more than you need them.

Work on you, everything else will fall into place.

Never resist change.

Step out of home & explore.

You & only you have to do it, less of expectations.

It takes time & courage & hard work to move on and realize your dreams. There is no shortcut!

My life would have been less if those rejections had not happened, because I would not have learned the lessons that are now shaping my life. They've made me stronger than ever.

What would you be willing to die for?

I won't ever die, since I am not just a being but a creation of this universe and energy is neither created nor destroyed, but only transformed. I will keep transforming till this universe is here.

20 November, 2015

Who on the planet is living the life you dream of living and what is it about their life that speaks to you so deeply?

Though there are many people around the globe who are living extraordinary lives, but I can never compare my life to others or others to mine since we have different goals and visions. Everyone is unique. I just imagine myself–living the life of my dreams, inspiring and changing lives all over this planet by making them realize–the hero in you.

What will you no longer tolerate in your life?

Anything that is not in order with my dreams. Wasting time in useless activities, mere thinking not doing, and zero tolerance to negativity.

29 November, 2015

If there was one thing you could change in your life to lift it to its highest level, what would that one thing be?

Not change but I would like to improve.

That one thing would be-defining my goals, then short term goals with deadlines, and accomplishing them with all my might and a super positive attitude.

If I had 30 days left to live, what would I do?

I would–

Finish writing my book "The Night I Woke Up" and speed up the process for its publishing (which actually didn't happen as you can make out).

Eat healthier and exercise on a regular basis so that i can see myself in shape again. (somewhat near)

More care and affection to my lovely parents and my loved ones.

Will take care of my beauty regimen strictly.

Will travel to the most beautiful bakeries in India.

Will go for spa and aroma therapy.

Would feed dogs and help build a shelter for them. (The best part)

If the five people you spend most of your time with were asked how they would describe you as a human being, what would they say?

As motivating, cheerful, grinning, always talking about dreams, having a positive aura, and saying that everything's possible. (I hope I haven't exaggerated!)

1 December 2015

If your tombstone could have one line on it, what would that line say?

She lived her dreams and inspired billions of others to realize the hero within.

5 December, 2015

What would the child you once were think of the adult you've become?

The child I once was must be astonished and surprised to see me as a beautiful, elegant, a positive and a confident leader. (It's ok to be a little self-obsessive. No?)

How old would you be if you did not know how old you were?

5 years old.

What do you want your life to look like in every area (career, personal, spiritual) 24 months from now?

24 months from now, my career would be blooming like I could never imagine. I would already have 3 international best-sellers on my name and having changed billions of lives, loads of business offers at hand, motivating and inspiring at top high notch venues. Wow!

My personal life? Mum and papa both, are so happy and proud of me. My master mind alliance grew into millionaires. "discover the hero in you" grew into a multi-billion dollar business. At spiritual front, I am in love with myself more than ever. Every morning, I wake up into a more beautiful me, to inspire my universe, to love animals and help underprivileged, and go to sleep with utter satisfaction and love. Pure love.

Which 5 things make you happiest in life?

Being on stage and performing like a hero.

Pouring out in my journal.

Exploring bakeries and cafes.

Loving animals and helping underprivileged.

Inspiring people and helping them discover their infinite potential.

To buy new pair of shoes, bags, clothing, and accessories (I could not rub out this one)

Who do you most admire in your life and why?

I admire the person i see in mirror every-day. I admire the way she smiles when she looks at herself in complete awe every morning despite of her tangled hairs and the loose pajamas. I admire the butterflies she has in her stomach before going on stage and knowing the fact that she had always dreamed of having those butterflies. I admire her eyes when she looks at the street dogs with so much love and affection. I admire her for every time she stood by the dreams and the vision only she could see. I admire her for the way she is.

If an 18 year old asked for your finest advice on life success, what would you tell her?

I would tell her–before you know what success is, know thyself. Know your passion, your purpose for being here, what you want, what you don't want, what kind of a person you are and what kind of a person you want to be. Know yourself so well that you become your own god. Then you would be successful.

Introduction

The idea of writing this book came when I had finally decided to follow my dream, but like many of us, I did not have the slightest idea of where to start from?

That magical day, I had just finished reading a book and the last sentence that I read was–

"Start from wherever you are and whatever you have! But start."

I knew I have something inside me that needs to be shared.

You are holding in your hands, not a story but an experience that will challenge you to hold on to your dreams till you realize them and question your everyday reality and the purpose of your existence.

All serious stuff? Don't worry. It's going to be very informal and frank. This is the way I am and I urge you to feel easy and look at the experiences, observations and ideas written in this book, in their true light. I have written this book with a commitment to bring and see the change.

I'm sure it is going to start with you.

Let's peel back the onion as to how it begun.

Chapter 1

Stage? No Please!

June 23, 2013-my fourth semester of engineering. It was during the time of my summer training session.

(You hardly get a month after the semester exams to relax and bring yourself back to the normal state when the college again comes up with kind of, another scheme to ensure engineering students remain in a constant state of abnormality)

Sitting on the second desk of the first row from right and cursing me for not being absent that day. There was an ominous silence prevailing on the faces of my poor classmates, including the terrific speaker, the well-known-"Me."

I had recently gained the fame among my college mates for having lost eight kilograms and looking better than ever and now, my well recognized impression was in danger.

The trainer was decreeing the students to get ready to be slaughtered, so that when he would call anyone randomly, the "poor children" don't fell unconscious out of anxiety.

It was the most dreadful, the nerve-cracking, the one and the only, EXTEMPORE! The scariest words-"Come on Stage. Yes you, looking at the back."

I don't understand why suddenly, everything goes into the slow motion? I was looking at my watch after every one or two seconds and then at the gate. "God…! Send that HOD (Head of Department) who speaks one thing in a hundred different ways to eat up the time and kick this man out. Help!" And this is one instance when your prayer is never heard.

One by one, the trainer was calling out the names. Sitting at my desk riveted with my heart fluttering and trying to watch the trainer from the corner of my eyes.

You just feel like, if you had DORAEMON you could have disappeared in a second using The Anywhere Door. All sort of thoughts were bubbling inside my head.

"Next is Shweta Singh…" It was my turn. I wish I was dreaming.

Out of nerves, here I was, standing miserable before sixty nine students to give an extempore on Women Empowerment. More than anything or anyone, I needed to be empowered at that moment. I think, not even my own ears could make out what I was trying to speak, "Umm…blah…ahh…I am here to speak on…" let alone the audience.

Unbelievable, the panic!

Did you just recall your own jittery experience at school or college when the word "stage" gave you goose-bumps?

It was not the first time. Every occasion, I had to face a staring audience (even 5 was large for me) to give a presentation or speech or perform any stage activity, I would go through nightmares during the day.

"Am I the only one?" I wondered.

I would pray for the earth beneath my feet to collapse and take me in for the sake of the innocent audience, and of course, I did not want to look stupid.

Though it was funny at times but heart-breaking.

The truth is you might laugh at yourself before your friends and mates, only to hide the embarrassment. Somewhere inside, you feel the sheer helplessness.

Who doesn't wants to speak well, stand confident & express oneself fear-less?

For me, it was a DREAM. I wanted to feel the excitement, the passion and the confidence I could see in others.

I would carefully watch other students, especially girls, who would speak with poise and were able to express their ideas with utter confidence.

I would actually admire them, for it was a near impossible thing for me.

Their legs did not shiver like mine did, nor did they eat up the sentence before it was complete.

I would dream of myself, being on the stage, "performing like a Rock star and speaking like a Hero " (Dreams can be too dreamy at times).

I would dream of the day when my legs won't be quivering and I will speak like I always wanted to.

Perfect body posture, eyes brimming with confidence, appropriate voice modulation and a pleasant smile. Everything–just perfect.

I would imagine, my classmates coming to me after my performance, and saying, “Shweta! You speak so well! How do you do it?”

And when everything seems perfect, that’s when you call it a *Dream*.

It wouldn’t take much time for me to wake up to the reality. The reality was–I was an introvert and an unconfident dreamer. I would sit at one corner (you must have had a favorite corner in your school or college) of the class and speak to a very limited number of people who were more or less, like me.

I did lack the confidence, to stand up for myself (even when a few of my so called friends would make a mockery of my chubby appearance in the first year) or to engage in conversations, or just start one by myself.

It was hell difficult for me. I even dreamed of getting a job where I won’t be asked to speak much. I mean, I was too much!

Despite the trouble and the disappointment I could feel, I never took it seriously, until one day…

It was another impromptu day, a session at “Communication Skills Enhancement Program.” To me it seemed more of a “Nervous Breakdown Program.” I was leaning to one side of my desk as if mice trying to enter the hole inside the wall. Unfortunately, there was none. *Or maybe, fortunately?*

I was perplexed. Should I try and raise my hand this time? Or no! I won’t be able to do it. Not again.

At one moment, I would try to take my hand out from the pocket and reach an inch raising it, and the next moment would take it back.

Only fifteen minutes were left for the class to get over. "Should I or should I not?" I mean what? I was awfully nervous. The trainer asked, "Who wants to come? Anyone?" as if she knew I wanted.

I closed my eyes and took a deep breath. I felt if not now, then never! I could not make out, all of a sudden, what made me pull my hand and push it against the force of gravity up in the air. Maybe fake confidence could help this time?

The applause made me even more conscious. My legs were shaking as if an earthquake was hitting the floor as I was walking towards the front. At least, I gathered the courage to make a fool out of myself. Standing there, I realized it was a big mistake. I was tight lipped–THUNDERSTRUCK! Again!

I garbled and fumbled. Maybe, this wasn't enough.

A group of boys in the front row began to scorn. Their laugh put a full-stop to the half-eaten words that were coming out of my mouth. Looking at their disgusted faces and then at the class, I went blank. The trainer, however, trying her best to suppress her mock, offered a glass of water to comfort me. The day…! It was 4th September 2013.

Well, it wasn't funny at all. At least not for me.

While on my way to home, my mind was playing a super bomb movie, a non-stop reiterate (just like the while loop does in C++) of those hilarious twenty minutes and asking me, "Why the hell you want to be a slapstick comedian?"

As I reached home, mommy opened the door. She didn't take a second to ask me the reason my face was booming like a balloon. I mean HOW? No matter how much you try to conceal, she always gets to know. Mom is mom. Agree?

Well, I didn't say anything except that I was feeling a little exhausted.

It was 8:30 pm. Looking into the mirror and combing my hairs, "Well done Shweta, at least you are an entertainer on stage whose act is designed to make an audience laugh…" I said while trying to act deaf to the mocking-laughter of the boys, still echoing in my ears.

That night I could not sleep. But I made a promise.

Did I take that laughter and the embarrassment to heart? Completely.

Was raising my hands really unfortunate? Let's see.

HAVE YOU EVER FACED ANYTHING LIKE THIS? HOW DID YOU FEEL?

WHAT DID YOU DO THEN? WAS IT ACKWARD FACING THE SAME PEOPLE THE NEXT DAY?

I did not want to continue being mediocre anymore.

You just cannot let go everything that happens to you.

I began my search for a place to reinvent myself. A place where I could learn to speak my heart out, overcome my stage terror and bring the big within me out on the face.

Shortly afterwards, I joined a public speaking institute.

My journey had already begun.

JUST A THOUGHT-

Why do we rarely have MEN EMPOWERMENT as a topic for discussion? What do you think?

Chapter 2

The Face Off

January 4, 2014-my first day at the public-speaking institute.

It was for the first time I was travelling to a place other than my college. While in metro, I was reading the book–*Life Lingua.* The foremost book I read other than my schoolbooks, dreadful engineering books and champak (the best ever).

As I read-

"If you have built castles in the air, your work need not be lost. They are where they should be. Now put foundations under them."

And the stop came.

I was a little late. I just waved off the metro station like a storm. I was rushing up the stairs of the building like a squirrel.

And then, this was it.

A completely new and different atmosphere it was. In fact, I was in a different world. I could feel the positive energy brimming in the air as I entered the class." What a multifarious sight!"

People from doctors and engineers to interior designers and business-men, from housewives and news reporters to politicians and diplomats, from almost all professions, had gathered for one cause-to face their fear of PUBLIC SPEAKING.

I was actually, astonished.

"And I was thinking that I am the only one…"-a sigh of relief.

The class was about to begin. "Were they waiting for me?" I thought.

I was a newbie and was trying to get myself comfortable in the new space when, the trainer, called me on stage to introduce myself to the class.

"What!!" I was right? They were actually waiting for me.

My heartbeat grew to the speed of a bullet train.

To add more to the growing anxiety, I was to be fired with a hell lot of questions regarding my career, hobbies, studies and what not.

It was too scary!

"How would I be able to respond to all of them?"-I murmured.

"I hope am not looking plump…" as always, an overdose of looks consciousness took a toll on me. I buttoned my leather coat and waved my hairs to one side.

I was nervous, but at the same time, a bit excited for a new beginning–A Quest Towards a Better me.

I knew I could not step back now; for it was the very reason I was here.

I walked to the podium and stood there. All twenty seven (see, I remember) pair of eyes was goggling at me.

For a short while, I felt as if, a staring contest is going on between me and the audience, like who will blink first. Later, they started giving me looks of an army who was ready to attack.

While we were busy staring at each other, I made up my mind to try my best to retaliate.

It was getting interesting. Standing on the top of the mountain and my heart rate increasing with every second, I began with a brief introduction.

I spoke of my interests-that I make one of the finest coffee in the world (my sister would throttle me if she reads this), bhangra lives in my soul, my love for baking and how I wish to speak in the coming days. What all values I live by and my desire to bring about "something" wondrous and magnificent.

But what was that something and how was it going to come to culmination?

I cracked one or two jokes on me and narrated the crazy incidents that happened a few weeks ago.

Whooaaahhh…how could I do that? It was not a normal thing for me to do, since I always found myself around the bend, while facing an audience.

I realized, laughing upon yourself; eases your nerves and makes you feel really comfortable and open. It acts like an ice breaker.

(Though there are always some people who would still try to rack your nerve by pointing out irrelevant questions to make you feel like a dumb hole, but atleast this time I completed my sentences and made my audience laugh for a good reason)

I was amazed. It was not that bad and difficult as I thought it to be.

While on my way back home, travelling through the metro and recalling those superb fifteen minutes on the podium, I felt having made a progress. For it was the first day, I spoke and didn't feel broke. I knew I was on the right path.

Your feelings show you the way.

I would eagerly wait for those two days. Saturday and Sunday. At every session, there were new people to interact with and new challenges to meet.

Be it story telling or role-plays, memory enhancement techniques or voice practices, it was fun. Absolute fun!

But was it just about having fun and interaction? Was it about speaking well?

How can your biggest fear turn into a fun filled activity?

WHAT DO YOU THINK?

Chapter 3

With Dreams in Pocket

Every day I had to face the stage.

The sight and the feeling are so lively when each person out in the audience is just gazing at you, hoping you to deliver something stupendous and sensational.

The place that once gave me goose-bumps now seemed familiar. I actually, stepped out of my comfort zone. I did things that scared me.

"Until and unless you run towards your fears, you cannot grow."

I noticed a change. I stopped giving energy to things that did not matter anymore.

Life started changing as I grew from inside. Till a month ago I used to feel helpless, ignorant and sympathetic for myself.

It took a bit of courage to look beyond my self-imposed limitation, a pinch of embarrassment and a mug overflowing with a desperate feeling to transform, when self-love and respect arrived in my life.

I would talk more, often start off a conversation by myself, and reach out to people with much needed confidence.

"When you gain self-confidence, it is like sowing a seed of belief. By nurturing it every single day, you nurture that belief which makes you grow from inside."

I was growing and so does my interest in public-speaking. I enjoyed being on stage with every inch of my body.

I do not remember having won any competition or any prize in my entire school life (except in pre-nursery for reciting a poem on mike). It was here I won one after another.

I won the third prize in the second public speaking championship I participated in. And in the next, guess what? I bagged the first. That trophy was a mark. A mark of a better me. When I touched that trophy with my bare fingers, it was not less than a dream.

I slept with the golden trophy wrapped in my arms for three consecutive days.

(Though now I understand, nothing materialistic can ever be a mark of your progress or accomplishments. The person you actually become is the true mark.)

I was being called "The Future Public Speaker" more than by my name. I cannot even put down those feelings into words. It was that amazing.

It was hard to believe.

"Confidence and self-belief when mixed in right proportion, act as the ultimate magic wand."

I had always dreamt of speaking well and brimming with confidence. It was happening, right before my eyes.

And the ultimate feeling?

"When you walk past your fears and hold victory over them."

For the first time in life, I realized my worth. Finding your passion changes everything. I began loving myself more than ever.

Life seemed more beautiful than it did before. Just wanted if I could wrap my arms around *LIFE* and say, *THANKYOU!* My self-esteem reached a new level altogether. All areas of my life were blooming with happiness and tranquility.

Dreams? Yes! They do come true.

I was improving with each passing day.

I was a new person. Inside and outside.

Around four months later, I was being offered a job as a public speaking trainer at the institute I joined as a naïve speaker and as a professional content maker. Afterwards, in a yet to be established company from California and as a team mate with another entrepreneur. (I did not even know the exact meaning of the word *Entrepreneur)*

All of this, before I was even a graduate. I gave a thought or two, whether I was ready to take up any of them?

Though I did not know exactly what I wanted to become, certainly, none of these opportunities I found, was for me.

I knew one thing. I wanted to create something.

I wanted to craft my own empire.

I did not want to work for some-one else's.

I wanted to do something which people generally, are scared to do (though I never want to jump from a cliff or pick up a lizard by her tail neither I plan to do anything like this in future. No way!)

I was never interested in knowing what's happening around the world. I was just keen on knowing what's going inside me. *Then it all began.*

"What is the purpose of my life?"

"Who do I want to become?" these questions would often pop up into my head.

I was confused.

With the storm inside growing rugged and wild, it was becoming difficult to carry on my engineering (the most-hyped-only-option for helpless science students).

Let me decant out. I cannot miss this opportunity.

Be ready for a series of How, Why and What!!

I never understood, why do we have to get our practical files checked and get an alpha, beta or gamma (according to the date of submission, pathetic!) as if we are first grade students, and that too when the professor knows that the entire class has copied from one? I mean, what sense does this makes?

I never understood the reason behind learning derivations only to write *Hence proved* in the end? What about the alien invasions, Bermuda triangle and the more than 95% of the Universe that we know nothing about?

I never understood why the lecturers are called "the lecturers" when they too teach from notes in hands and if asked a question outside the syllabus, they would immediately give you a hard look and turn to the board saying, "*this is not in your syllabus. Let me complete your syllabus first.*"

It is not just in colleges but school too. Syllabus, assignments and the most devilish of all–Marks! Chant and focus on just these three words and you would be labeled as an educated person. This is worth giving a thought.

Well, "Marks and Grades" are the real culprit.

Our education system encourages following masses than being unique. And then we study the reasons for ***Lack of Opportunities*** in India under Social Studies.

Can you recall how many formulae, you were told to practice a dead minimum of hundred questions on, during your board exams have helped you in the time you were depressed or were in real trouble? Can you?

Does holding a degree means–You are qualified for an exam called ***Life***?

You are taught on *"how to become a topper"* more than *"how to become happy and a successful person."* (Yes they do come hand in hand)

You are given *"extra classes"* for practicing previous years might come questions rather than giving focus on your personality growth and mannerisms.

Is this the reason people say that life starts after you become a graduate.

Because by the time you are a graduate, you hardly get a moment out of making practical files and giving exams to look and introspect what you really want to do?

Then you don't seem to have the time to think about your passion and dreams because you must do something to earn else you are (in our biggest well-wisher *society's* eye) a useless creature.

I am waiting for the day when *The Human Mind, Power of Imagination, Discover your Purpose* and *Happiness* will be the main subjects of schools and colleges, besides practical learning of physics, math and chemistry.

Just imagine, an educational institution where young people would learn to do practical things, and at the same time develop their minds!

I never wanted to take up engineering, but then I didn't know what I wanted. This is the case with most of us. Since every second person of the science stream was opting for engineering, I did just that. A perfect nomad I was.

I never introduce myself to anyone, as an engineer. I am just a B.Tech graduate who is engineering her dreams.

I would dream of the person I wanted to become the entire day and then at night would take up the previous year papers when exams would approach. And some of my friends were always skeptical about how I studied for two days and still managed to get 76%?

Somehow, I made it to the end.

Well, isn't it strange?

When you don't have a purpose to live and to strive, you are like a rudderless ship with no idea where to go. What do you think happens to a rudderless ship? It is bound to sink! And so is your life.

You don't have a direction. You wake up every morning, doing the usual chores, go to bed and you keep repeating this abyss of boredom, until one day; you have a break-through moment of insight.

This is the moment you realize-You are here to make a difference. A difference not only in your own life, but in the life of others!

Living one more day as usual seems as if you've spent another day being ordinary.

I wanted more and more people to know–If you have the courage to dream, then you can achieve them too. That dreams, really come true; like mine did.

Amidst all the questions and confusions bubbling inside, I had this vision to inspire people.

Like many of us, or like you, I too wanted to make a difference.

But how?

If you were at my place, what would you have done?

From where would you have begun?

Which person would you have reached out to?

What is the first thing coming to your mind while you are reading this?

Chapter 4

The Boundless Boundaries

It had been just 6 months. I got to know myself more than I did in nineteen years, right from my birth date, altogether.

WHEN YOU SEEK YOUR INNER SELF, YOU START BUILDING A RELATIONSHIP, WHICH UNFORTUNATELY, MOST PEOPLE DON'T HAVE THE TIME TO!

You discover a whole new world of opportunities. You discover that your dream world is on the other side of your comfort zone.

Moreover, when you recognize your core area (things you are good at and you love to do), it seems almost impossible to engage in never-ending gossips, chatting online for hours and involving in ZERO-VALUE OUTCOME activities. Yes I am pointing to all the stupid stuff that we keep doing. Trying to kill time by being online on Facebook and Whatsapp for long hours and draining your energy alongside, opening up people's profile to check their latest pictures and updates (To be honest I used to do this once but not now), watching TV serials and that one thing which people are obsessed with–p**n. These are *Life* destroyers.

Pay attention to when, where and how many times your fingers linger to get onto that shiny and attractive piece of glass ensemble on a circuit. It won't take time for your "window to world" to turn into a "cage without a key." Remember this.

But the moment you become aware of where your time and focus is going, you begin to transform your habits.

Just a belief, self-realization and moment of break-through can create so much difference.

I was sailing through in the river of dreams, completely in love with what I achieved. But somewhere inside, I was scared.

"Will my family approve of my decision? Will they allow me to follow my dream? How will everyone react? What if I hurt them? Will they talk to me afterwards?" questions put forth day and night.

What I could listen to my heart singing all these months, was not in order with what I was supposed to do or I should say, expected to become.

I remember being a kid, I was told (and not asked) to join the prestigious Indian Civil Services. Not only my parents, but my entire family always had big hopes and mountain reaching expectations from me. Whenever any relative would come to my place and ask–"what will you become when you grow up?" without giving a second thought, I would jump and say, "an IAS officer!" Not even a single person did ever ask me, "Why do you want to become what you want to become?"

From my late maternal uncle to my beloved grandfather, everyone in my house wanted me to become a high rank officer in the Indian Civil Services.

From my play school to introductory class at the public speaking institute, I created a buzz about me going into Civil Services. At that time, my dreams had not arrived in my life.

But do you think a kid understands who an IAS officer is or what responsibilities he or she carries?

There is this peculiar thing, especially among typical Indian uncle and aunties, when they hear about an Engineer, a Doctor, a diplomat or an MBA, there eye-brows grow taller, eyes an inch wider (from both corners) and they look for insignificant ways to get their daughter or son hitched as if people in these four professions come with some super-natural powers?

And the moment you tell them about you being a writer or a blogger or a traveler or a chef or an artist and not from the earlier mentioned four hyped professions, they would look (superciliously) at you with so much disgust that you literally would think for a moment and wonder, "Is I DO NOTHING inked on my forehead?" How interesting!

Next time you happen to introduce yourself to someone who is a die-hard fan of the conventional career options, observe the facial expressions. You'll realize you are on the right path.

There was a fear of losing all the attention and pampering I used to get when I was being talked about as the future IAS officer and not getting the same for my aspirations.

When I got an insight into my purpose and discovered the love of my life, more than being excited, I was scared.

I feared of not getting the support I needed for bringing my fantasies onto this world.

Just have a look around. You will find your friends, your cousins and a hell lot of people, who are merely getting ready to live but are not actually living. They are surviving, but not thriving for the lives they intend to create.

What according to you can be the reasons? Lack of focus? Lack of facility? Lack of opportunity? Lack of motivation?

Does a child need a personal car or I-phone or a debit card?

What about appreciation and encouragement to create their own lives?

It doesn't matters much if you fail twice or thrice, or if people ridicule you saying-"You idiot! You know, your dreams are way too big to be realized. So get off them!"

If your family is with you, apparently, you have that inner strength that keeps your morale high.

But the real picture in our country, as wonderfully put forth by Dr. APJ Abdul Kalam as–

Children must be encouraged to follow their dreams and create their own lives. But unfortunately, they are told to become like everyone else.

"Don't fly in air! Keep your feet on the ground." Familiar?

Does having dreams and the desire to make them your life label you as a CRIMINAL? I think, certainly, because this is the present scenario, at least in our country.

I hardly read newspaper. I hate it actually. Whenever I get my hands onto one, I come across one or two cases of suicide. Most of the times, it is about students who committed suicide as they could not stand their family's expectations.

It obviously doesn't means, one should run away from the problems and involve in such an act of cowardice, but it does affects one in ways that cannot be comprehended.

(Let's go off the track)

It's time for you to think!

If you love doing math, can you ever be stressed doing excess of it? (Though I know, math might be an alien language for you, just like it is for me. PS. No offence) or if you love reading history, can you think of committing suicide just because you could not handle more of it?

You are loaded with tons and tons of expectations, not only from the family side but also from the neighbor of your neighbor.

Let me recall an eye-opening incident.

I attended a self-defense workshop in the final year of my engineering. The trainer, after introducing himself, asked us a question. He said-"Imagine a marathon of animals. A bird can fly, but a lion cannot. A lion can run and has excellent hunting skills. But a fish cannot fly nor it can breathe in air, but it has fins and gills to survive in water. What about giraffe, insects, reptiles, carnivores, herbivores, omnivores and the remaining ones?"

He continued…"Can we put all the animals in the same marathon? Will it be fair to make them compete with each other in the same marathon?"

Not even a single person sitting in the hall could answer. I guess I know what you're thinking. Each and every animal has distinct features and unique abilities, which make them perfect for one activity and not so perfect for another.

Am I right?

Every animal has at least one unique ability which makes it different from the other animals.

If we cannot put them in the same marathon, why are we participating in the same race to become engineers, MBAs, doctors, CAs or government officials?

I wonder sometimes, what could be the reason for these ever increasing unemployment rates?

I did go off the track, only to give you a glimpse of how fast we are heading towards a world where mere bodies will survive, not souls.

By the way, which world would you like to be a part of-A BROKE WORLD or YOUR DREAM WORLD?

Chapter 5

Welcome to Rejections

So, here I was, stuck in a catch-22.

"How should I tell my parents that now, knowing what I want my life to stand for, I don't want to prepare for civil services?" I was done with my final year exams. It was already a month sitting idle at home, thinking "what next?"

Almost every day, I would wake up with this thought to gather courage and talk to them about what was bothering me. I would start with-"Mom and papa, I wanted to say something…" and when both of them would stop doing the work and then glance at me, I would change the topic as if nothing happened. "What if this all turn out to be disastrous?" this thought was eating me up.

I wanted to get off this lumber, as soon as possible.

One day it went over and I just poured my heart out. I was never this scared facing my parents. Not even when I got 20 marks out of 70 (failed!) in physics pre-board in the twelfth standard.

My parents were talking for hours in the room, while I and my sister's ears glued to the little space left open between the gate and the wall.

After a long conversation and much to my surprise, they decided to give me a chance. "What? I mean what? Really?" I was elated.

It was as if a breaking news that spread like fire among my relatives and friends. "What is she doing?," "where is money in it?" Some would come to my face and say, "so you think you'll make a career out of it…holding a mike? Seriously? Join a good coaching for UPSC and start preparing." And you feel like, every other person is concerned for you, except you.

However, this was the moment I was waiting for. I was excited and ready to take up new endeavors.

I had already performed a motivational event DRMZ DO COME TRUE at my college. It was the first event of its kind, and it was organized by me. The feeling was unbelievably, awesome.

I did things; I never thought I could do. My first seminar and I managed to fill up the seats to the end of the auditorium. I was pretty confident of my voyage.

On a mission to ignite sparks into the lives of people, I created a facebook page "Discover The HeRo In YoU" and launched my own YouTube channel-Shweta Singh, where I uploaded self-help motivational videos, shot at home.

I messaged several societies and college associations to organize my events briefing up my purpose behind them. I thought it would be easy. "Why won't people call me if I am ready to speak for them?"

I don't even remember the number of magazines and newspapers I messaged to.

One week, two weeks and then a month. Many would appreciate the initiative and the purpose, but not even a single of them said-"Let's do it!"

I kept strong. I thought, maybe I should start with my school. It actually felt good to start my journey from the place my journey started.

There was still a hope. I decided to go and work out a plan for a guiding session with the school mentor. I wore red and blue check shirt, paired it with black trousers and tied my hair up. After all, it had been four years. I wanted to look all grown up and elegant. I took courage with me and then went to school.

The school building was looking even more magnificent then it looked at my time. The Principal must have had put in a lot of money for its renovation. After all, you judge a book by its cover. No?

As I entered the school reception, I felt a little nostalgic. I could see the teachers, who had once taught me, passing by. Nothing had changed. I was smiling and all the feelings and incidents just came alive before my eyes.

It was a great feeling. The mentor finally arrived. After a brief conversation, my event was finalized. My blogs were decided to be published in the yearly magazine. A cherry on the cake it was for me. I could not believe it. I literally pinched myself and jumped out of joy while stepping out of the school reception.

Only the date was to be finalized. Back home, I began writing the content and preparing presentations.

"I would be performing at the place, where I once used to sit in the audience as a student," this thought only was enough to make me come out of the bed every morning. Things again seemed to be working out.

It took almost a month, 6 books on adolescence and self-discovery while watching videos on an array of topics and I was ready for a power packed performance.

I was dreaming of my class teachers coming to me and saying, "We are proud of you Shweta." I was so excited for the event. I was out of sleep.

Amidst all the excitement and preparations, I almost forgot that The Universe has its own plans. Little did I know, it was another rejection on my way? No matter how many times I would message and ask for dates, the day never came nor did any response. There was no response, whatsoever. I could not gather enough courage to go to school again, since it would have been a question mark on my dignity.

"What went wrong?" I could not make out. Maybe, if I would have been a Bollywood star or some celebrity motivational speaker, they would have at least bothered to reply me. ***Fortunately,*** I was just a girl who believed in her dreams and in her school too.

Isn't quite strange?

When you are already a star or you've made a niche or already accomplish something great, your school and college immediately pops up with greetings and congratulations that–"This person got his or her schooling from OUR SCHOOL or GRADUATED from our COLLEGE."

But when the person is on the road to attain the goals, even the school that is proud of you (afterwards) fails to recognize you.

Will they ever encourage you to become a musician or an artist or a chef or fashion designer?

The answer is quite motivating.

I was again there, at the starting point.

Was I tensed? Yes, I was. Was I depressed? No doubt.

Nothing seemed to work out. Everything I tried collapsed, one after another.

It had been four months, and I could clearly see my beautiful world of dreams shattering down to pieces. "Are dreams meant to be dreams only?" "Did people say right when they said–your dreams are far from reality?" "Why is it so difficult convincing people?"

I wasn't prepared for such a setback. More than anything, I was scared of not having been able to prove what I always wanted to–that EVERYTHING IS POSSIBLE!

Was I really living in a figment of my imagination?

Another month passed away. I convinced myself or let me be more open, I forced myself into civil service preparation.

And what about my dreams? The chapter was closed.

Would you have accepted the breakdown?

Chapter 6

Life of a Zombie

There was a sigh of relief for my parents, for now, I had the security tag with me of being a "Civil Service Aspirant." It was quite obvious and apparent.

Besides, I would not forget to remind myself of the perks of being a civil servant, just to distract my mind away from the dreams, which were still haunting me.

"At least not happy but I would have a 9–5 secure job for lifetime once I clear this," I used to think.

I would get up in the morning, do the usual chores and then sit down to study. If by chance, I would look into the mirror, while walking and revising my notes, I did not like the person looking back at me. I would feel, as if I am cheating upon myself.

I lost the courage to look into my eyes. I did not try to question this feeling, for I knew, I did not have the answers, or maybe, I did not want to answer them.

Life came to a standstill. Life became opaque.

We spend our fourteen years in school reading without absorbing, cramming without questioning, writing to give exams, submitting copied assignments, and then when after gaining so much expertise and knowledge (you know what I mean...) we again repeat this cycle to get a job. Fantastic!

While scrolling down the Instagram feed, if any picture or quote about dreams would come, I would try to make my heart understand-"It is impractical. There is no truth in it. This is not for me!"

Nothing inspired me; neither had I looked at the world the way I once, used to.

"You change your thoughts, you change your world." Mine was a different case.

I was same (at least in skin), things in my bedroom were same. Only my perception was different. A lifeless perception. There was a feeling of listlessness and dissatisfaction which I had never experienced before.

I was clinging onto the branches.

I have always been good at academics, so I was confident to be able to clear the exam in the first attempt. My parents would be proud of me; I would become a well-known personality, high salary and much hype. But then again, a question mark. Was I happy??

"Whom should I go to and explain how am I feeling?- it was becoming unbearable. I did not want to tense my parents just because–I was not happy!? I already had committed the mistake of asking people and searching for the answers outside of me. *That made things even worse.*

I was not content. I was not satisfied with me and my life.

The fire I once felt inside, to create my dream life, to inspire and motivate people, to make a difference had gone astray to the core. I was close to a creature without dreams, without courage, without enthusiasm, without vision. I was close to a ZOMBIE.

Have you ever been to a ZOMBIE world?

Chapter 7

Let Me Take You There

Why are you taken aback?

You must be familiar with this place, since each one of us has been here atleast once. The only difference being, few return while many remain trapped here for lifetime.

Let me brief up on how this place looks like.

People here are breathing but they are not alive. They wake up without a goal and go to bed without satisfaction. They are always getting ready to live but don't seem to have the time to live.

They try and substitute time and affection with money and gifts. They place possessions before people. Can it be the reason-they are lifeless dummies?

They are totally out of dreams; in fact they don't have at all. They are living the pedestrian life given to them believing it as their fate.

These people are described, according to my Life phrase book, as ZOMBIES.

Some people unknowingly became a resident here. I really feel bad for them. Their only fault was–they had dreams but they came here and started seeking approval–what is right and what is not?

I heard them asking to other ZOMBIES–"Should I go for it?" "Ïs it safe and sound for me?" "Please I want someone to sustain me!" And when the ZOMBIES bombarded them with-"Are you nutty?" "You won't amount to much!" "You won't ever be able to make it!" They accepted these negative hetero-suggestions about themselves and in no time, they too twisted into ZOMBIES. Creepy?

Poor people.

I came across one more kind of ZOMBIES here. They are almost, everytime glued to their phone screens. Eating, sleeping, reading, driving, even when they have to go to p**p....ahh! They are inspecting their phones every now and then, sometimes just staring at their phone screens. Their eyes have a red tint due to constant exposure to the evil light. They might be sitting next to you, while you are busy talking to me. I know it's terrible to find them around you but don't run... one more category is left!

Did you ever hear or met a ZOMBIE who always keeps complaining about everything and is full of hatred and jealousy? Yes I am talking about the one at your workplace and in your class too. No matter how much they have, they are always hungry for more (they want shortcuts for everything).

What if! The Universe blessed them with a lovely family and friends; they feel an urge to be in the state of melancholy. What if! The Universe blessed them with healthy eyes to see the world and its colors while thousands of people in the world can only pray for it?

What if! The Universe blessed them with the ability to walk and travel the world while many are disabled? What if! The Universe blessed them with the ability to listen to the beautiful music life has to offer and serve with their two hands, still they feel a desperate urge to be in a state of depression. They are often quoted as saying-

"I don't look good enough!" "I am frustrated because I look unattractive!" "I wish I could look like him or her!" "I wish I was luckier!" Well, the sight is horrible.

Make sure if you find yourself in the ZOMBIE world or are somewhere about to reach, take your steps back.

It solely depends on you. WHICH WORLD?

Both are here on earth. If someday, you happen to meet any of the above described ZOMBIES, make sure you help him or her come out of the invisible yet dreadful world of hell.

And beware.

So, where was I?

Chapter 8

The Re-Incarnation

It was morning.

I woke up with the chirping of the birds that had made their nests on the back side of our balcony. They were tweeting without taking a breath. It was really soothing to hear.

I took my slippers and went straight into the balcony. Standing there and feeling the cool breeze on my skin while watching the birds leaving their nests and flying straight into the sky.

Weather…it was so pleasant.

The sky looked exceptionally beautiful. I kept gazing at the sky, the clouds, so many different shapes, the birds flying high and the lively shimmer of the sun.

I wondered if there's an end to the vast and seemingly, infinite and bravura blue sky? Where does it stop? Or does it? What's beyond we cannot actually see with our unclothed eyes?

The same day, in evening, I was going through a fashion blog by Kritika Khurana, during my twenty minute study break. "So many amazing things are happening in my life right now! Can't believe, all dreams are coming true," as I read. Was it for me? How happy she might be feeling while writing this? And,

Here was this question right before my eyes,

"What am I doing with me and my life?"

I felt choked. I was overwhelmed. My eyes burst into tears. I felt as if, all that was accumulated and wrapped under thick sheets of gloom and dismal, over the past few months, found its way through my eyes.

"Atleast someone is happy and living her dream." I thought, while crying. What made me sob my heart out? Maybe, I wanted to feel, what it really feels like when you breathe your dream. Maybe, wanting that "amazing things" emotion and not having it despite of trying? The dreams I once, wished to bring to this world, and the life I wanted to create for myself, flashed before my eyes, once again.

I kept sitting there, re-reading those beautiful words of her, flashing at my dim phone screen. It was almost midnight.

My eyes were burning with a deep feeling of resentment and exasperation.

I went to bed. As I lay down, my eyes fell upon the posters. The words were still shining, despite of the darkness in the room and my life. I felt as if they are saying-"You must believe in the power of your dreams. You can do it! You can do it!" My eyes were still hazy. There were my stunning golden trophies; standing with their mesmerizing charm and as if whispering-"You are here to transform all your dreams into authenticity. You are here to live the most miraculous version of yourself. Get up, try one more time and stop not till you achieve."

I closed my eyes, trying to forget that my soul felt barren. I landed in a state of oblivion. There was no pain, no feeling, and a nothingness of stillness for a moment that I will never forget. And then gradually, a feeling of centeredness.

I had never felt more connected to who I was. I felt a steadiness in my body and an admiration for existence that today I still cannot describe. I felt lifted from the shards of my life and deeply connected with THE UNIVERSE and the waves of azure streaking across in the night sky. I could hear the applause I always wanted to. I could see thousands of people who've just come to listen to me. I could hear the click-clack of my beautiful heels as I walked up the stairs, towards the stage. I could see a young girl with side ponies walk up the stage with a pen and paper. She is too excited. I could feel my fingers, wrapped around that majestic mike and my eyes, blurred with tears, and shouting,

"*You are a Hero. Thank you so much for all the love!*"

I can never forget that picture.

I had tried to travel the "logical" path three times before it was impossible for me to bear the load of cheating myself.

That night, I could not sleep.

For the last four months, I had been breathing my days, devoid of excitement, enthusiasm, zeal and passion.

Sometimes, I really speculate. How did I grow into this person who yearns for a passionate and a dream packed life? That night, I did lose my nap, but I found myself. I chose my intention and my vision over fake refuge and naysayer's talk. Earlier, I wanted to follow my dreams as I felt it would be amusing. This time, my dreams were the very air I wanted to breathe in for the rest of my life. This time, I made this choice out of pain.

Did I want to reach the end of my life thinking, I could have given myself and my dreams another chance? NO WAY!!

Wait! What about you?

Before it gets too late!

After 14 years of waking up at 6:30 am to returning home after 2:30 pm and then your tuition teacher ready to bang on your head, from making those useless posters and models for internal assessment (which most of the times, was done by our poor parents) to running after lecturers for half a mark.

From being glued to books day and night during boards, to making the project presentations (which were again from the market), from crying on not getting above 90% to praying just to clear all semester exams, I have, no we have come a long way.

You are supposed to do a lot of things. Things you don't want to do or even think about.

You are supposed to get a college degree, get some experience on a resume, position yourself for a career, and take a good paying job with a stable company.

And then…

What about your imaginings and desire?

They will happily accompany you to your grave and will forever rest in uproar. *Not in peace.*

Work you must, but on your dreams first.

Till the night I woke up to my dreams, I always let fear decree me. "What will happen if I fail?" "What would happen if I could not prove myself?" "What if am being rejected?" All of this happened. My fears caught me.

WHAT YOU RESIST PERSISTS.

I wasn't prepared to fail. I did take failure to heart and naysayer's talk to my head.

I had already been knocked down to my knees.

After that night, there was no fear. I had nothing to lose. The worst had already happened.

Though The Universe has a perfect plan for all of us, and every failure or setback you come across carries equal or greater opportunity and meets you for a definite reason, still, there's a lot you can learn from other's experience.

After all, life is too short to take on life's every lesson by committing the mistake, all by you.

But before you start, keep this thing in your mind-it's not going to be easy. Especially if you happen to choose an alien profession, like me.

The start is always a bit difficult. *It takes time to become immune to non-craziness.*

Why is it difficult? Well, just think, if it would have been easy, everyone would be doing it.

How many times did you set out to conquer your dreams, but then, one thing after another went wrong? You know what the problem is? We think it is over! We fail to look beyond a small stupid failure. You fail to realize, just like the universe which is present beyond the blue sky under your head, is not visible to your eyes, you have talents that are hidden in your day to day activities and abilities that you cannot even imagine or comprehend.

What if we start exploring ourselves, our known and unknown talents, just like the world beyond the sky? Life would be magnificent, beyond imagination. THINK.

Failure is the price paid for ambition.

-Robin Sharma

Before you set out on your journey, ask yourself, if you are ready to pay that price.

Before you think of success, you must make up your mind for the challenges that will no matter how much you'll try to resist will adorn your path. They are the very jewels that carry the luster and shine, to brighten up your life, once you start labeling them as opportunities and not difficulties.

As far as I have observed, from my experiences, more than 90% people cannot walk this phase.

Challenges signify two things for me. First, it signifies that you are trying and taking enough risks (which are not actually risks), you deserve the salute for. Second, life is testing you to check if you really, are committed.

The most important lesson-Do not hold anyone responsible for your life but you. Your parents, your family, your friends, your colleagues, your partner, no one is responsible for your present circumstances but you.

As I said in my book "7 Incredible ways to Gorgeous failure!"–

It is your journey. Do not expect anyone to take a stand for you, if you don't have the moral fiber to stand for yourself.

You cannot say-"This man or that person did not allow me to go for my dream."

Our parents are just concerned for us. They do not want us to struggle. They don't want to hear our dreams but see them alive. They want to see results. Work on your dreams and show them. I can bet you'll need a camera to capture their expressions when you show them that mom and papa, *this is what I did!*

Next - Don't try to meet everyone's expectations. It's not your job.

Things don't always go well. It happens to everybody. A dry spell is no fun for anyone, but it's often only the extreme situation that gets us to look at ourselves: to find out that what we're doing, why we're doing it, and what needs to change to get the best possible result.

What may at the moment seem like the end of the world won't seem so important in seven days or in seven months or in seven years. Take the long range view and you can't be defeated by momentary setbacks.

You must believe in yourself, despite of the adversities.

I lacked that self-belief and commitment when I started.

Your failures are the glorifying marks (and not school grades) of your progress. They clearly signify-You are doing something!

Your crashes are the ingredients of your evolution, as well as a mark, you are progressing. I learnt.

Failure is a temporary detour, not a dead end. It is something we can avoid only by saying nothing, doing nothing, and being nothing.

It takes persistence and total commitment to your goals, but it's possible.

The whole meaning of any setback–or any success, for that matter–is how we take it or make of it.

We often look at high achievers and assume they had a string of lucky breaks or made it without much effort. Usually the opposite is true, and the so-called superstar or "overnight success" had an incredibly rough time before he or she attained any lasting success.

Live your dreams in your mind first, keeping your eyes closed. Visualize your highest self. This vision will keep you going when at times, there seems no way out.

The picture of THE BEST VERSION OF YOU must be before you every moment.

I am the person of my dreams today.

The Universe seems to throw itself on the side of people who know exactly what they want, if they are determined to *get just that!*

I used to say, "Shweta, yes, you are starting out small; everyone has to. But you have a powerful message, and you need to share it with others. You have learned a lot in life, and you can inspire others. You are going to help billions of people some-day. Today is the day; just keep working at it. You are bigger than any of the obstacle that might come in your way because your dreams have no limits."

Remember that all good results come slowly. While you are waiting for the big break to come, do not lose sight of your vision, how important your dream is and how many you will serve one day.

The way I speak and handle the audience (with utmost humbleness) was once a dream for me. I have successfully published my E-book *"7 Incredible ways to Gorgeous failure!"* Having a book on my name was once a dream for me. What you are holding in your blessed hands is my dream. I only used to talk about it while strolling in the book stores and book fairs. It is a reality now.

But this won't stop me from improving and getting better and then very soon… The Greatest Motivational Speaker in the world history, to inspire and motivate billions of people like you to live their dreams. This is my dream.

It's time that you think for yourself.

Think back to a time in your life you have found difficult. Try to see what you gained as a result of what you learned, what strength you found even in the most trying time–or what strength you find now in your having overcome it.

Perhaps you may never have been aware of what you gained until you think about it now.

Living through painful experiences, we can become stronger people.

The transformation depends on your ability to discover something beyond the pain.

I wanted to share my story as a message to you that no matter where you are, no matter what you have got, no matter if initially it seems impossible to you, you can always dream much bigger than your present circumstances. And the good news is, you have everything in you to become the person you dream of.

Yes, you are powerful beyond your imagination.

Words from a Friend...

Once upon a time there was a girl
Scared to face the realm
too ordinary for this world
she was not like others...
She was different
And for this crime she was forsaken
Since her childhood she was made to follow
the safe path in life
But she dreamed to walk the road not taken
One night she stopped the sounds echoing
inside her mind.
Voices telling her that she could not do it...
She decided it was enough...decided to stop
this entire fuss...
Realized that her existence was for a purpose...
That night she hopped out of her comfort zone and
started to let her thoughts flow
She fell and got up
Drowned and swam
Wounded and healed
Hurt and learned
That night She began to grow
She grew into something extraordinary...
something special..
She became special not just for the society...
but in her own eyes

She always knew what she really wanted…
now she started to believe..
"There is nothing we cannot achieve if we follow our
dreams"
A phrase she started to not just chant repeatedly…
but change she started to feel…
That night she turned this feeling into an attitude…
a plan…a way of living…
A plan to step up and bring a change…
Not just in herself…but in every human being…
She was not scared anymore,
Not scared of the thorns that lay on this road
henceforth…
Not scared if it was dark ahead or she would be alone…
She was prepared to face the worst…
Yet her optimisms knew no bounds…
She had a spirit to help others find a light…
In times when there is darkness all around…
One night…that was the night…that has made all the
difference…
The night she came out of her cocoon…
The night she jumped down the tree…
Out of her comfortable nest…only to go back up…
And every day that followed was a miracle…
like flying in the magical sky…
After that night back in time…it was the night
she woke up.

Will You?

Do you have the courage to stand up and commit yourself to your dreams in the face of adversity?

Will you believe in the unseen, when no one could see it?

When you feel like quitting, do you have the guts to get up and remind yourself the reason you started?

Will you?

Can you dare to say "Yes I will?"

It's Very Personal

Life is a gift. Follow your dreams. Live every moment as if it's your last. Live your passion.

Do what you love. Take your own decisions.

If you can convince yourself that you are born to accomplish wonders, then you can convince anyone, let alone your family. The best part is that you don't need to convince, you need to show them the results. Your parents and family is always there for you, but if you won't believe in yourself, how can you expect them to believe in you?

Don't fear anything! What? Why? How? Just take a step in faith. Everything else will follow. The Universe has made all of us. We are a part of this creation. You cannot even make out how much pain and struggle we had to go through before we came out here in this world, only to live a purposeless and an ordinary life? No! Absolutely Not! You are a stunning success because you are alive.

Find your joy. Never be afraid to express yourself. Never be afraid to be you. Everything is possible, only if you want it bad enough. Don't try to be someone you are not. Don't aim to be one in billions, because you are exceptional & matchless in this entire Universe. You are The only one.

Let your dreams, happiness, joy, passion, awesomeness, liveliness, abundance, love, faith, power, potential, confidence and vision take a toll on you. Allow yourself to be completely drenched in your own love. Love every single inch of your body. Love the person you see in mirror, kiss and pat yourself, jump and swirl around for this life is so precious.

I cannot express in words my feelings as I am writing this. I feel if I could just pop out from this book and tell you how special you are to you, to your parents, this world, this Universe, that how much you matter and how your dreams can change this world!

Then You Must Fail!

If you ever fail in your life, fail to give up!

If you ever fail in your life, fail to give in to the circumstances that once knocked you down!

If you ever fail in life, fail not to remind yourself every moment that you are a hero in your own world and no matter how much it takes, you've got more than what it takes!

You'll be proud that you failed!